DEEP BLUE BREATH

Story by

Clay Beabout

First published by © Make A Film Foundation 2011
Printed in the United States of America.
This book is printed on acid-free paper.
ISBN 978-0-9845779-6-5

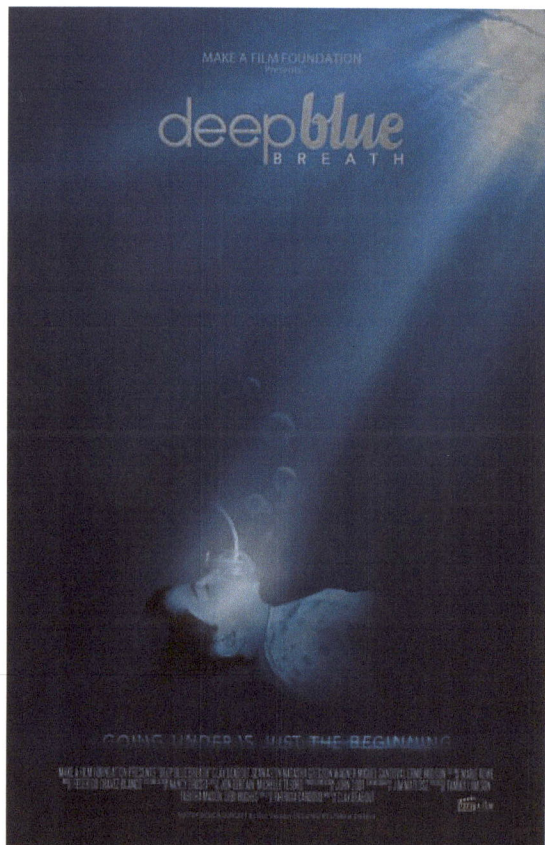

Based on the short film "Deep Blue Breath"

Story by Clay Beabout
Adaptation by Cleve Lamison
Storyboards by Bob Foster
Art & Animation Stills by Six Point Harness
Layout & Design by Terilyn V. Lawson
Lord Vater Costume & Weapons by Davis Fandino at Studio ADI
Fish Wall Paintings by Terry Ziegelman
Photography by Michele K. Short

Live Action Characters:
Clay - Clay Beabout
Dad - Sean Astin
Mom - Natasha Gregson Wagner
Doctor - Miguel Sandoval
Lord Vater - Michael Phillip Edwards
Charger - Charger

Special Thanks to:
Titanium Rib Foundation: titaniumribfoundation.org
AmyLou Designs: toothfairypillow.net
Brendan Burch & Ryan Samsam - Six Point Harness
Alec Gills, Tom Woodruff, Jr. & Davis Fandino - Studio ADI

Make A Film Foundation teams children who have serious or life-threatening medical
Conditions with film industry professionals, who help them create short film legacies.

For more information, or to donate, please visit our website at:
www.www.makeafilmfoundation.org.

VATER Syndrome

V.A.T.E.R. Syndrome refers to five different areas in which a child may have abnormalities: Vertebrae. Anus. Trachea. Esophagus. Renal (kidneys) add (L) for limbs or (C) cardiac conditions changing acronym to V.A.C.T.E.R.L.

The hospital wallpaper always reminded Clay of the ocean.

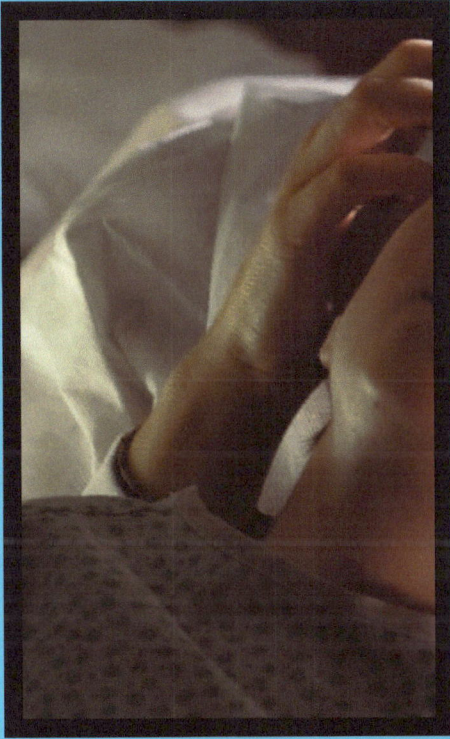

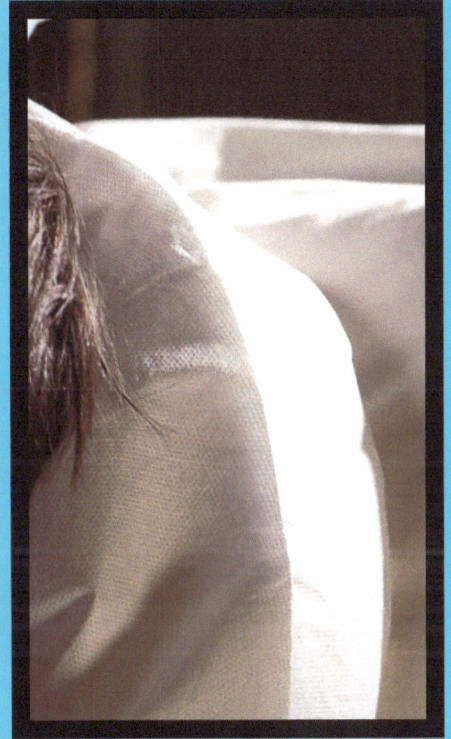

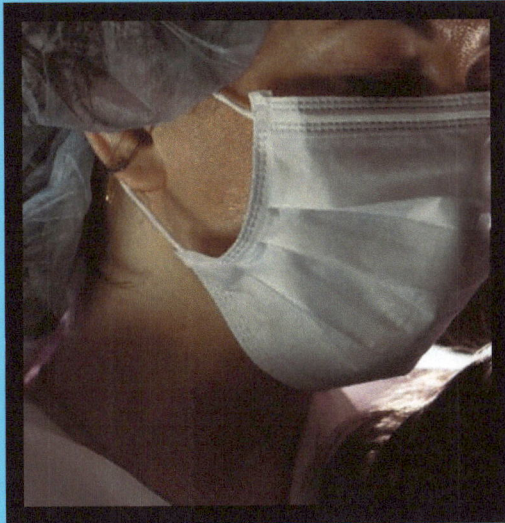

Clay had Vater Syndrome which made his body weak. But nothing could weaken his spirit. While the doctors fought the sickness in his body, Clay would need to fight the Vater with his spirit. But first, he needed to sleep.

WORLD OF DREAMS

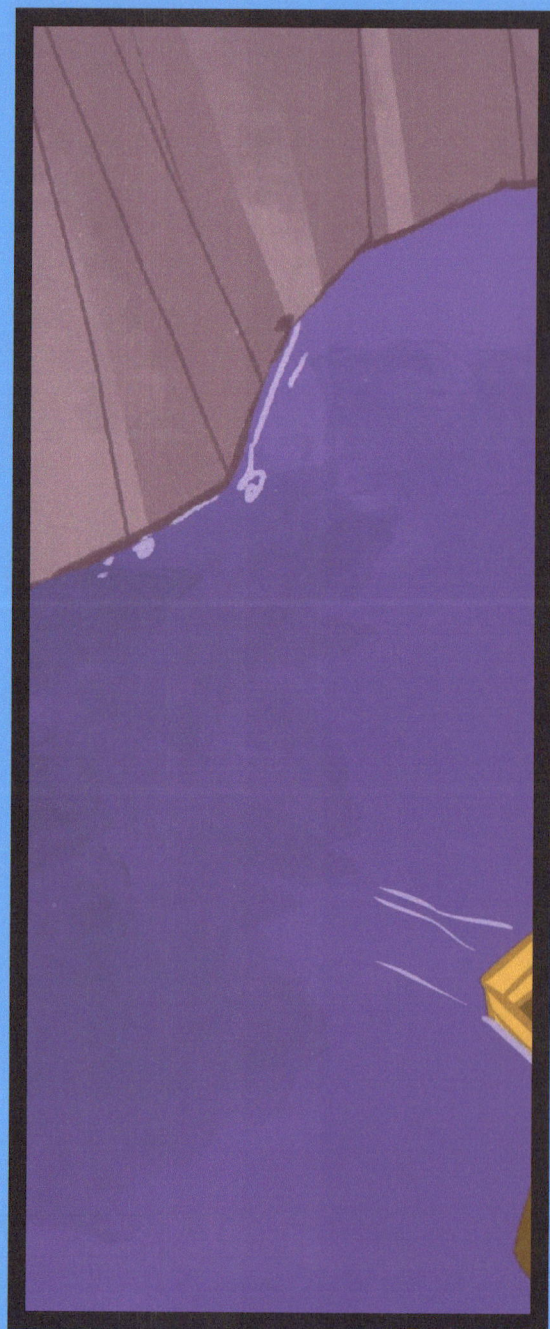

The sickness was deep inside of Clay.
He had a long journey ahead of him.

Clay saw many strange and wondrous things on his journey.

Like clouds that had funny shapes.

Some things were scary.

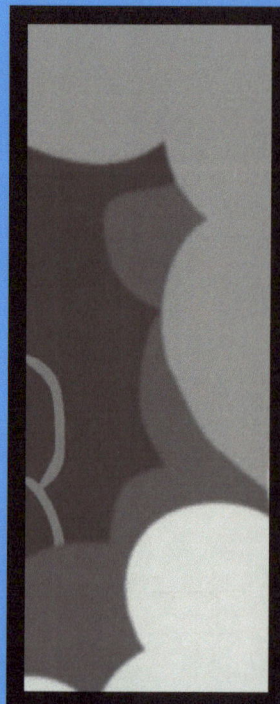

Some were friendly.

Clay, "What's your name? Do you have a name?"

Clay, "No? Well, I'll call you, Charger."

Land of Clay's Body

Clay, "Wow, Charger. I didn't realize how beautiful it is inside of my body. I think I should check it out. Pretty cool so far."

Clay, "The doctors are trying to fix me. I can still taste the bubble gum gas from the mask. It's sweet."

Clay, "Feels almost like I'm chewing it."

Clay blows a huge
bubble that lifts
Clay and Charger
into the sky.

Clay, "Wow! Let's go, Charger!"

Clay, "Look, Charger! A town!"

Clay and Charger land in the crumbled town.

Clay, "Whoa. Something terrible happened here."

Clay, "Hello? Is anyone here?"

Clay, "Look, Charger! Everyone's down there fighting!

Clay, "Hey! Why are you guys fighting?!"

The Evil Kuk-Nuks and Brave Tunas Battle

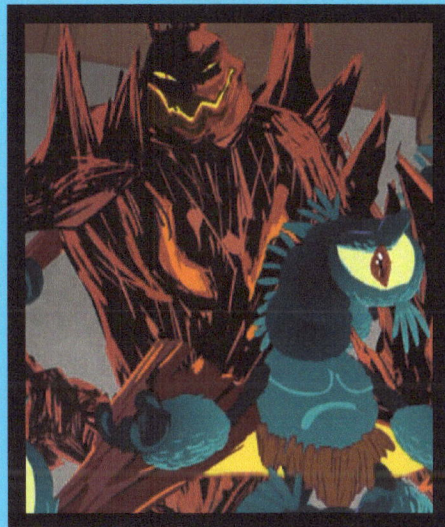

Clay, "Uh-oh. They're coming after us! Run Charger! Run and hide!"

Lord Vater emerges.

Lord Vater, "Foolish boy! Did you really think you could escape me? I am Lord Vater! And I will ravage this world!"

Clay, "What does ravage mean?"

Lord Vater, "Destroy! I will destroy it all! Bwaa-haa-haa!"

Clay, "Stinking disease! You're in my body! So I'm in control!"

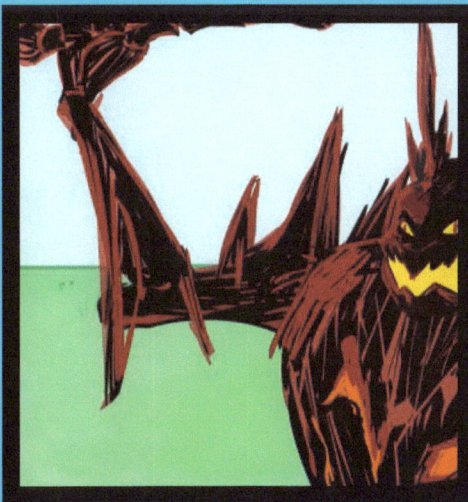

Lord Vater, "That's what you think!"

Lord Vater, "Aaaaah-hahahahahaha."

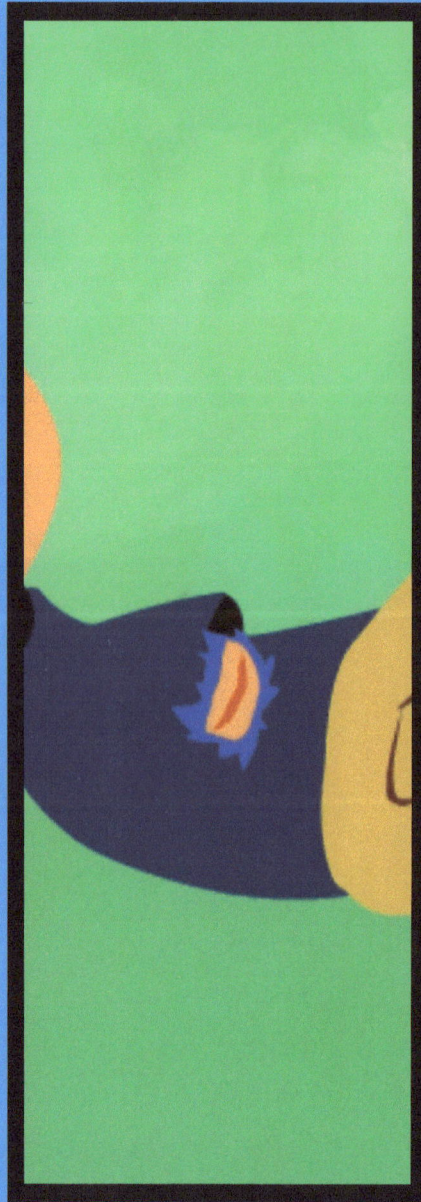

Lord Vater attacks Clay with his weapon. Clay, "Ugh! Help!" Clay is wounded.

Charger rushes in and chomps onto Lord Vater's weapon.

Lord Vater, "Oh no! Give me that you flea bag!"

Charger, "Grrrrrrrrrrrrrrr!! Ruff ruff!"

Clay, "Good boy, Charger!"

Lord Vater, "Get that mangy mutt!

The Kuk-Nuks grab Charger.

Clay, "Oh no. I'm losing my strength. I don't know how long I can keep up this fight."

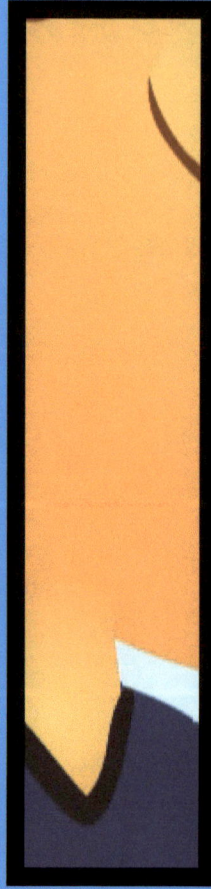

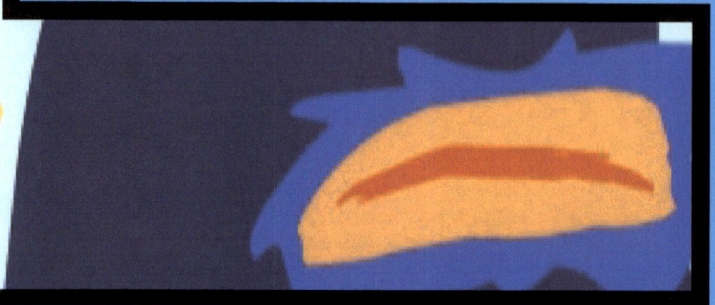

MEANWHILE, IN THE WAKING WORLD...HOSPITAL ROOM

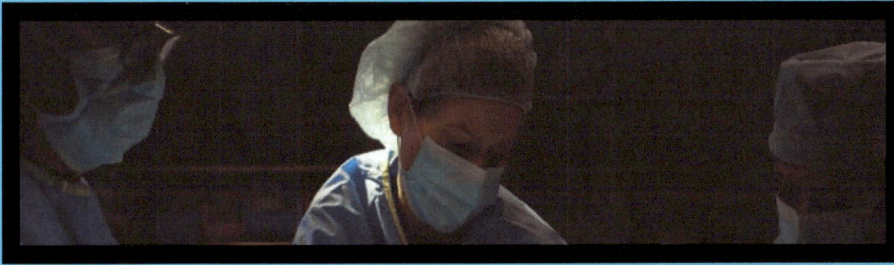

Doctor, "He's getting weaker! Get the defibrillator!"

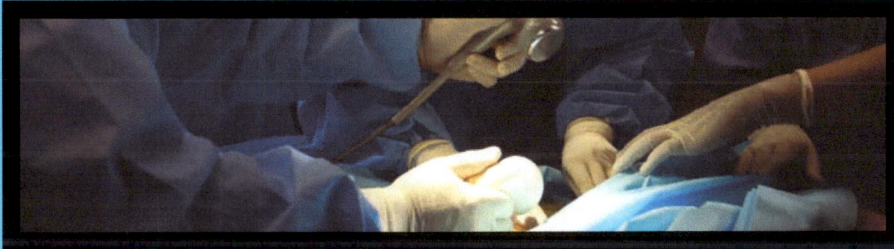

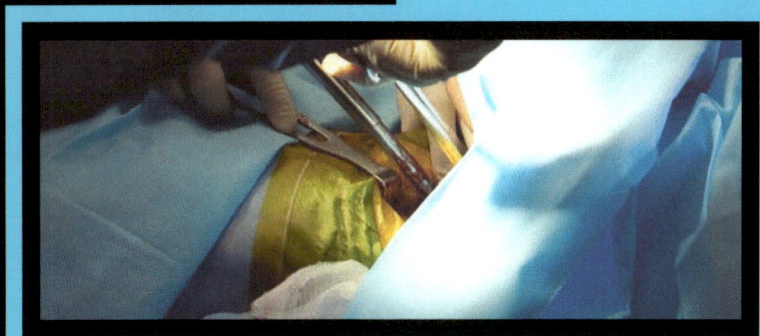

Doctor, "Clear!"

Chief Tuna, "Tunas attack!"

Chief Tuna, "Eat this evil-doers!"

Tunas step in to help.

Clay, "Thanks for the help, guys."

Kuk-Nuks, "Eeeeeekk. Aaaaarrrk."

The Kuk-Nuks' bodies dissolve into blood.

Clay, "What kind of ammunition was that?"

Chief Tuna, "Vitamin pellets. Kills Kuk-Nuks every time!"

Clay, "Hey! I'm getting better!"

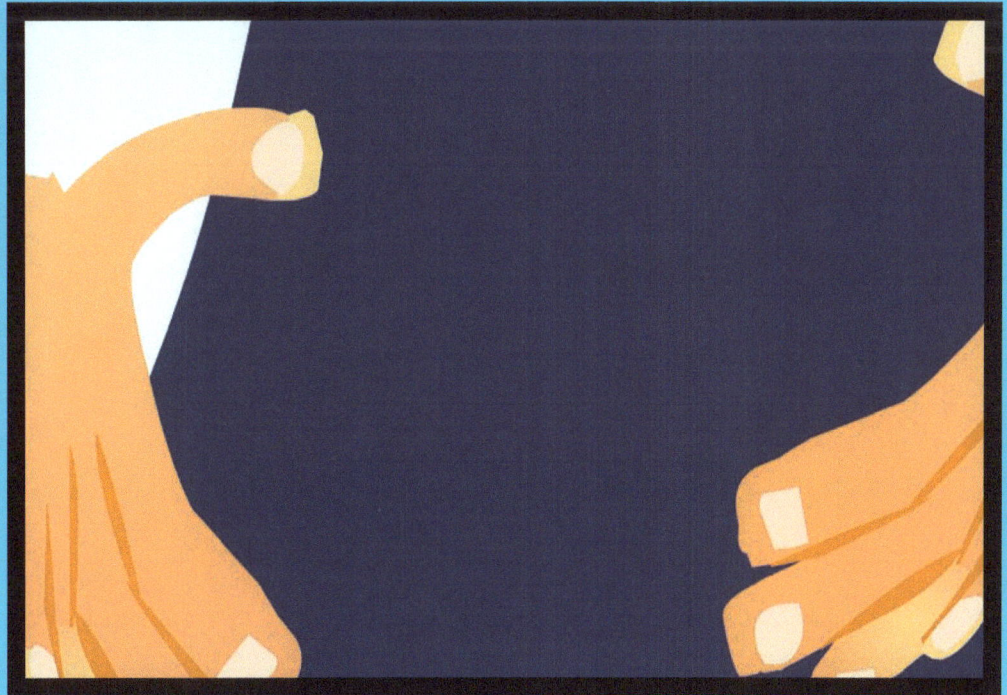

Clay, "My wound has healed!"

Lord Vater attacks Clay.

Lord Vater, "Not so fast! You can't take out Vater that easily."

Clay, "Ow!"

Chief Tuna, "Run, Clay... run!"

Clay, "No running this time. I'm going to fight!"

Clay grabs the Titanium sword.

Clay, "Eat this!!!!!" Clay stabs Lord Vater.

25

Lord Vater, "I'm melting! Meeeeeellllllttttiiiiinnnnnggggg...."

Lord Vater dissolves into a gooey mess.

Clay, "You're not the wicked witch, I'm not Dorothy, and that's not Toto!"

The Chief and the Tunas triumphantly surround Clay.

The Tunas celebrate.

Tunas, "Hooray!!!"

Chief Tuna, "The doctors can fight for your body, but the most important fight comes through your spirit."

Lord Vater is defeated.

Clay, "Yep. With a little help from my friends. Goodbye...and thanks again."

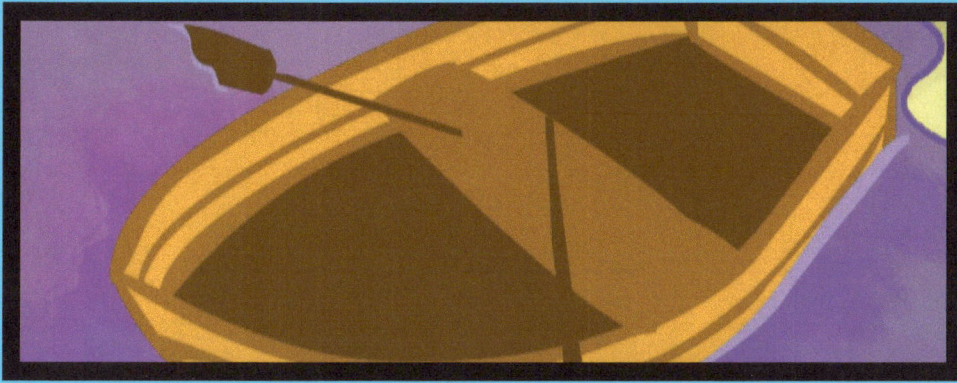

Clay, "Well Charger, I guess this is goodbye."

Charger, "Ruff! Ruff!"

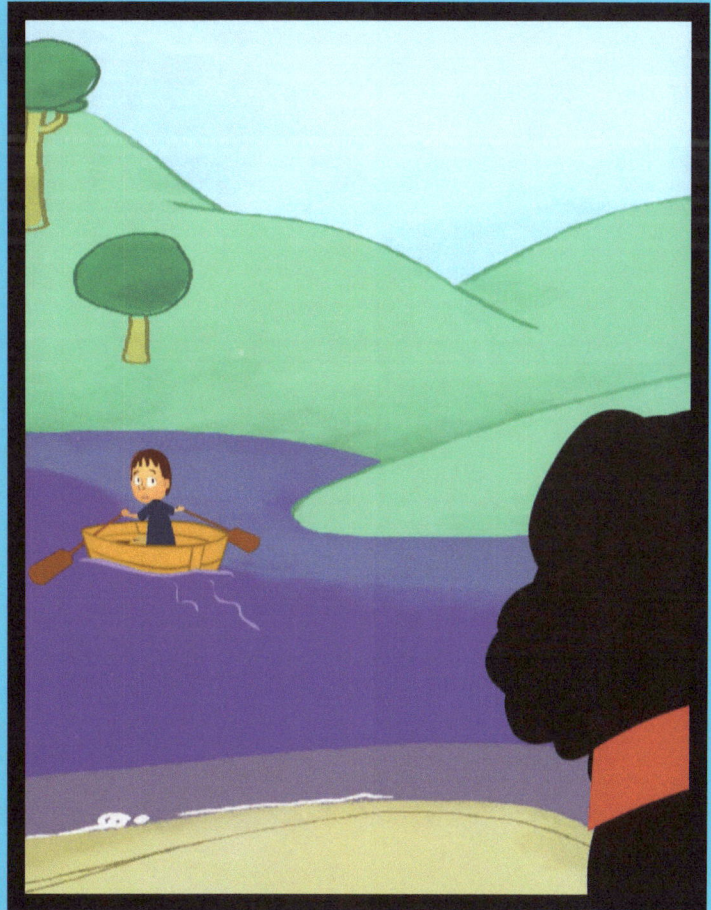

Clay, "I'll never forget you, boy!"

Dad, "Clay?"

Mom, "Sweetheart?"

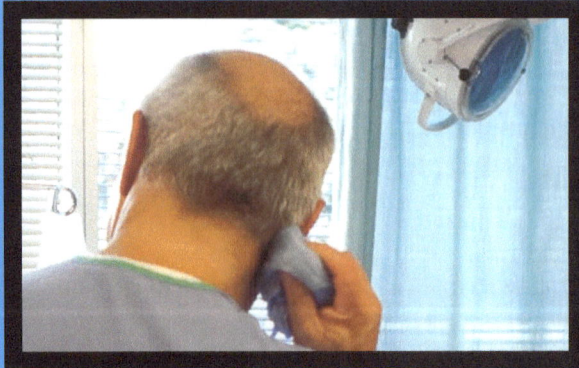

Doctor, "You're out of the woods now, Clay. Come on, wake up."

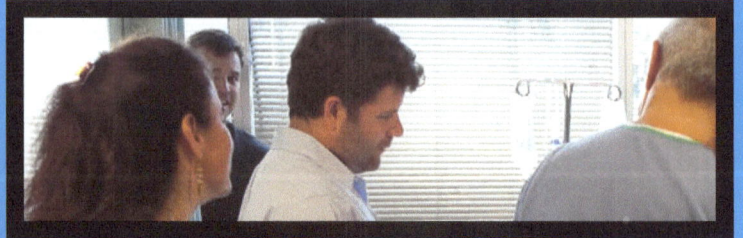

Mom, "We have someone we'd like you to meet. Clay?"

30

Clay, "Mom. Dad."

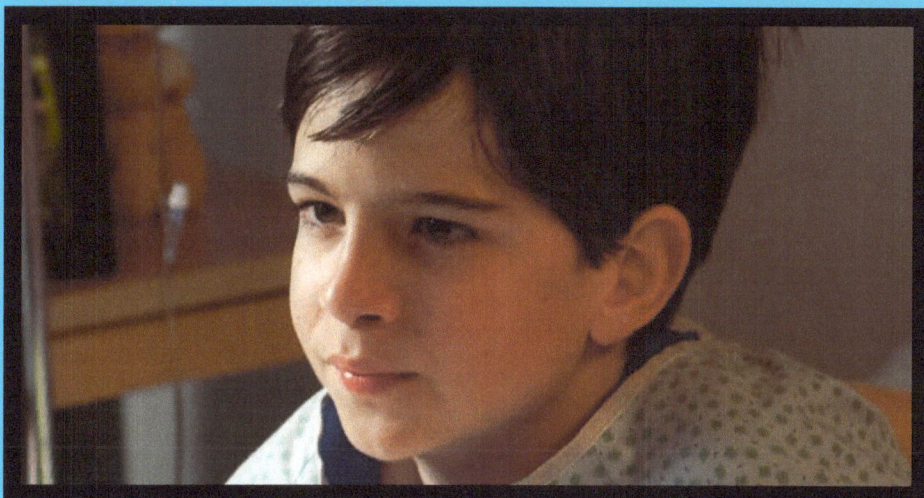

He sees his old pal.

Clay, "Charger!"

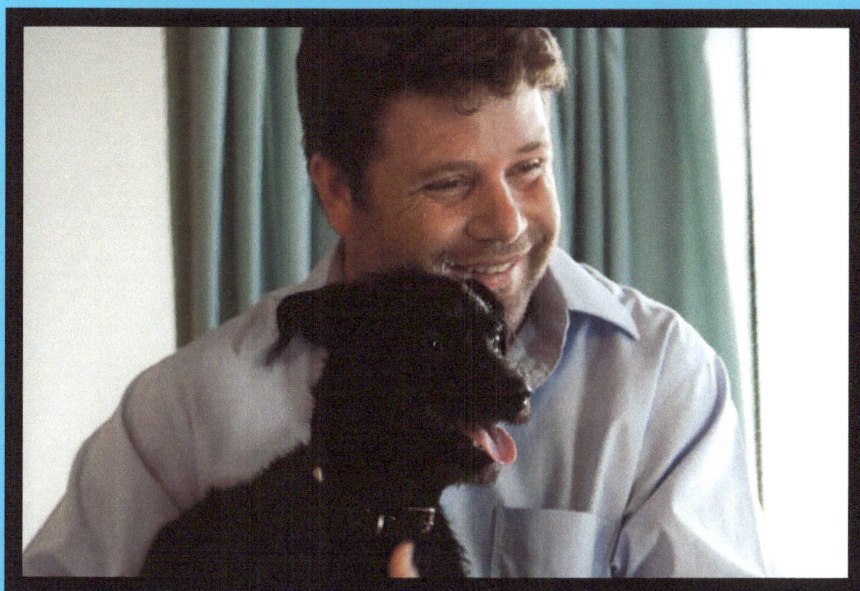

Dad, "Wow! It's like you two already know each other."

Clay, "That's cuz we do."

THE END.

www.ingramcontent.com/pod-product-compliance
Lightning Source LLC
LaVergne TN
LVHW072110070426
835509LV00002B/99